Phillieology Trivia Challenge

Philadelphia Phillies Baseball

**Phillieology Trivia Challenge – Philadelphia Phillies Baseball;
First Edition 2009**

Published by
Kick The Ball, Ltd
8595 Columbus Pike, Suite 197
Lewis Center, OH 43035
www.TriviaGameBooks.com

Designed, Formatted, and Edited by: Tom P. Rippey III & Paul F. Wilson
Researched by: Tom P. Rippey III

For information on ordering this book in bulk at reduced prices, please email us at pfwilson@trivianthology.com.

International Standard Book Number: 978-1-934372-54-8

Printed & Bound in the United States of America

10 9 8 7 6 5 4 3 2 1

Tom P. Rippey III & Paul F. Wilson

Phillieology Trivia Challenge

Philadelphia Phillies Baseball

Researched by Tom P. Rippey III

Tom P. Rippey III & Paul F. Wilson, Editors

Kick The Ball, Ltd
Lewis Center, Ohio

This book is dedicated to our families and friends for your unwavering love, support, and your understanding of our pursuit of our passions. Thank you for everything you do for us and for making our lives complete.

Dear Friend,

Thank you for purchasing our *Phillieology Trivia Challenge* game book!

We hope you enjoy it as much as we enjoyed researching and putting it together. This book can be used over and over again in many different ways. One example would be to use it in a head-to-head challenge by alternating questions between Phillies baseball fans – or by playing as teams. Another option would be to simply challenge yourself to see how many questions you could answer correctly. No matter how you choose to use this book, you'll have fun and maybe even learn a fact or two about Phillies baseball.

We have made every attempt to verify the accuracy of the questions and answers contained in this book. However it is still possible that from time to time an error has been made by us or our researchers. In the event you find a question or answer that is questionable or inaccurate, we ask for your understanding and thank you for bringing it to our attention so that we may improve future editions of this book. Please email us at tprippey@trivianthology.com with those observations and comments.

Have fun playing *Phillieology Trivia Challenge*!

Tom & Paul

Tom Rippey & Paul Wilson
Co-Founders, Kick The Ball, Ltd

PS – You can discover more about all of our current trivia game books by visiting us online at www.TriviaGameBooks.com.

Table of Contents

PHILLIEOLOGY TRIVIA CHALLENGE

How to Play

Book Format:

There are four quarters, each made up of fifty questions. Each quarter's questions have assigned point values. Questions are designed to get progressively more difficult as you proceed through each quarter, as well as through the book itself. Most questions are in a four-option multiple-choice format so that you will at least have a 25% chance of getting a correct answer for some of the more challenging questions.

We have even added an *Extra Innings* section in the event of a tie, or just in case you want to keep playing a little longer.

Game Options:

One Player -
To play on your own, simply answer each of the questions in all the quarters, and in the overtime section, if you would like. Use the *Player / Team Score Sheet* to record your answers and the quarter *Answer Keys* to check your answers. Calculate each quarter's points and the total for the game at the bottom of the *Player / Team Score Sheet* to determine your final score.

Two or More Players –
To play with multiple players decide if you will all be competing with each other individually, or if you will form and play as teams. Each player / team will then have its own *Player / Team Score Sheet* to record its answer. You can use the quarter *Answer Keys* to check your answers and to calculate your final scores.

1

The *Player / Team Score Sheets* have been designed so that each team can answer all questions or you can divide the questions up in any combination you would prefer. For example, you may want to alternate questions if two players are playing or answer every third question for three players, etc. In any case, simply record your response to your questions in the corresponding quarter and question number on the *Player / Team Score Sheet.*

A winner will be determined by multiplying the total number of correct answers for each quarter by the point value per quarter, then adding together the final total for all quarters combined. Play the game again and again by alternating the questions that your team is assigned so that you will answer a different set of questions each time you play.

You Create the Game -

There are countless other ways of using **Phillieology Trivia Challenge** questions. It is limited only to your imagination. Examples might be using them at your tailgate or other professional baseball related party. Players / Teams who answer questions incorrectly may have to perform a required action, or winners may receive special prizes. Let us know what other games you come up with!

Have fun!

Spring Training

1) When was the nickname Phillies officially adopted by Philadelphia?

    A) 1882
    B) 1894
    C) 1912
    D) 1935

2) What are the Phillies' official colors?

    A) Blue and Red
    B) Red and White
    C) Navy Blue and Burgundy
    D) Red, White, and Blue

3) What is the name of the Phillies' home stadium?

    A) Veterans Stadium
    B) Lincoln Financial Field
    C) Citizens Bank Park
    D) Kauffman Stadium

4) What year did the Phillies play their first-ever game?

    A) 1876
    B) 1883
    C) 1889
    D) 1894

Spring Training 1-Point Questions

5) What year did Philadelphia sign Pete Rose?

    A) 1978
    B) 1980
    C) 1983
    D) 1985

6) In which division do the Phillies play?

    A) AL Central
    B) NL East
    C) NL Central
    D) AL East

7) How many times have the Phillies won 100 or more
    games in a season?

    A) 0
    B) 2
    C) 4
    D) 7

8) Who has the longest tenure managing the Phillies?

    A) Charlie Manuel
    B) Jim Fregosi
    C) Burt Shotton
    D) Harry Wright

9) Was Ryan Howard drafted by the Phillies?

  A) Yes
  B) No

10) What was the purchase price of the Phillies franchise in 1981?

  A) $8 million
  B) $20 million
  C) $30 million
  D) $47.5 million

11) Who was the Phillies' opponent in their most recent World Series appearance?

  A) Tampa Bay
  B) Cleveland
  C) Boston
  D) Chicago

12) The Phillies have won the National League Pennant greater than 10 times.

  A) True
  B) False

13) What was the nickname given to the 1950 Phillies team?

    A) Young Bloods
    B) Wild Ones
    C) Phillie Floppers
    D) Whiz Kids

14) What is the name of the Phillies' costumed mascot?

    A) Phillie Phanatic
    B) Phil
    C) Furry Philly
    D) Philster

15) Citizens Bank Park has a seating capacity over 50,000.

    A) True
    B) False

16) Who is the Phillies' current manager?

    A) Ramon Henderson
    B) Steve Smith
    C) Jimy Williams
    D) Charlie Manuel

Spring Training

17) Who did the Phillies play in the 2008 Divisional Series?

 A) Cubs
 B) Dodgers
 C) Brewers
 D) Mets

18) What year did the Phillies play in their first-ever World Series?

 A) 1915
 B) 1932
 C) 1941
 D) 1950

19) Who holds the Phillies' career record for games pitched?

 A) Turk Farrell
 B) Ron Reed
 C) Tug McGraw
 D) Robin Roberts

20) Who hit the most home runs for the Phillies in the 2008 regular season?

 A) Pat Burrell
 B) Ryan Howard
 C) Chase Utley
 D) Jayson Werth

Spring Training

21) With what team did the Phillies share Shibe Park?

   A) Stars
   B) Eagles
   C) Athletics
   D) Fury

22) How many World Series have the Phillies won?

   A) 1
   B) 2
   C) 4
   D) 6

23) How many total runs did the Phillies score in the 2008 regular season?

   A) 799
   B) 821
   C) 839
   D) 850

24) Did the Phillies win greater than 95 games in the 2008 regular season?

   A) Yes
   B) No

Spring Training *1-Point Questions*

25) Who is the only Phillie to win the National League Most Valuable Player Award three times?

    A) Ryan Howard
    B) Jim Konstanty
    C) Chuck Klein
    D) Mike Schmidt

26) What nickname did the Phillies go by during the 1944 and 1945 seasons?

    A) Athletics
    B) Royals
    C) Blue Jays
    D) Mets

27) Did the Phillies have a winning record at the mid-season break in 2008?

    A) Yes
    B) No

28) What is the name of the area behind center field at Citizens Bank Park?

    A) Ashburn Alley
    B) Phillie Way
    C) Slugger Field
    D) Memorial Park

Spring Training

29) Was Jim Bunning selected as an All-Star every year he played with the Phillies?

    A) Yes
    B) No

30) All-time, in how many tie games have the Phillies played?

    A) 20
    B) 33
    C) 48
    D) 99

31) Who was the last Philadelphia player to win a Silver Slugger Award?

    A) Chase Utley
    B) Ryan Howard
    C) Mike Schmidt
    D) Bobby Abreu

32) When was the last season the Phillies lost greater than 100 games?

    A) 1923
    B) 1946
    C) 1961
    D) 1988

Spring Training *1-Point Questions*

33) Which Phillie great is currently a U.S. Senator?

    A) Steve Carlton
    B) Mike Schmidt
    C) Jim Bunning
    D) Robin Roberts

34) What is the Phillies' record for consecutive games with a safe hit?

    A) 36
    B) 38
    C) 44
    D) 56

35) Who was the last Phillies player to win a Cy Young Award?

    A) Steve Carlton
    B) Terry Mulholland
    C) Curt Schilling
    D) Steve Bedrosian

36) Which Phillies pitcher had the most wins in 2008?

    A) Cole Hamels
    B) Scott Eyre
    C) Brett Myers
    D) Jamie Moyer

Spring Training

1-Point Questions

37) Who is the only Phillie to hit four home runs in a single nine-inning game?

    A) Chuck Klein
    B) Mike Schmidt
    C) Ed Delahanty
    D) Mike Lieberthal

38) Against which NL team did the Phillies have the best winning percentage during the 2008 regular season?

    A) Colorado
    B) Atlanta
    C) Washington
    D) San Francisco

39) How many times has a Phillies pitcher won 20 or more games?

    A) 30
    B) 42
    C) 53
    D) 60

40) What was Rich Ashburn's nickname while playing for the Phillies?

    A) Whitey
    B) Golden Child
    C) Mr. Dependable
    D) Runnin' Richie

Spring Training

PHILLIEOLOGY TRIVIA CHALLENGE

41) Which Phillie had the most RBIs in the 2008 World Series?

    A) Jayson Werth
    B) Carlos Ruiz
    C) Ryan Howard
    D) Pedro Feliz

42) How many times have the Phillies scored greater than 1,000 runs in a season?

    A) 0
    B) 2
    C) 4
    D) 7

43) Who is the only Phillies pitcher to throw a perfect game?

    A) Kevin Millwood
    B) Tommy Greene
    C) Jim Bunning
    D) Rick Wise

44) How many Phillies were selected to the 2008 All-Star Game?

    A) 1
    B) 2
    C) 4
    D) 6

PHILADELPHIA PHILLIES BASEBALL

45) Who is the only Phillie to hit a grand slam in the postseason?

 A) Mike Schmidt
 B) Pat Burrell
 C) Ryan Howard
 D) Shane Victorino

46) What were the most Phillies selected as All-Stars in a single season?

 A) 2
 B) 3
 C) 5
 D) 7

47) How many Phillies managers lasted one season or less?

 A) 6
 B) 10
 C) 14
 D) 18

48) How many hits did the Phillies' pitching staff have in 2008?

 A) 22
 B) 38
 C) 45
 D) 57

49) What is the nickname of the AAA team affiliated with the Phillies?

A) BlueClaws
B) Iron Pigs
C) Phillies
D) Threshers

50) When was the first season the Phillies had a winning-record against the Mets?

A) 1962
B) 1969
C) 1973
D) 1976

Spring Training Phillies Cool Fact

Phillie Phanatic is one of the most recognized team mascots in all of sports. This big green hairy creature has been named #1 mascot in sports various times and became part of a permanent exhibit in the National Baseball Hall of Fame in 2002. The idea of a team mascot emerged in 1977 after a team executive saw the San Diego Chicken. The team paid $250,000 for the copyright of Phanatic in 1983, which could have been bought for $1,300 before his debut five years earlier. Known for razzing visiting teams, Phanatic pushed Tommy Lasorda to the limit in 1988. During a Dodgers trip to Philadelphia, Phanatic stomped on a dummy with a Lasorda jersey. Lasorda later called the front office to no avail. The next time the Dodgers were in town, Phanatic once again dressed a dummy with a Lasorda jersey and began stomping on it. Lasorda took action and slammed Phanatic to the ground. Unknowing to Lasorda, Phanatic was getting Lasorda's jersey from none other than the Dodgers star second baseman Steve Sax.

Spring Training Answer Key

1) A – 1882 (Team owners chose the word based on the city where the team is located. The Phillies hold the professional sports' record of longest continuous play in the same city under the same name.)

2) D – Red, White, and Blue

3) C – Citizens Bank Park (The stadium opened in 2004. Citizens Bank paid $57.5 million to have the naming rights through 2028.)

4) B – 1883 (The Phillies lost 3-4 to the Providence Grays on May 1, 1883.)

5) A – 1978 (Rose signed as a free agent in 1978 and first appeared on the Phillies' roster from 1979-83. He recorded 826 hits during his time in Philadelphia.)

6) B – NL East (Along with the Atlanta Braves, Washington Nationals, New York Mets, and Florida Marlins.)

7) B – 2 (The Phillies finished 101-61 in 1976 and 1977.)

8) D – Harry Wright (10 seasons, 1884-93)

9) A – Yes (He was selected by Philadelphia in the fifth round of the 2001 MLB Draft.)

10) C – $30 million (The Carpenter family bought the team in 1943 for $400,000 and sold it 39 years later to a group of businessmen for a 7400% gain.)

11) A – Tampa Bay (The Phillies won the series 4-1 against the Rays in 2008.)

12) A – 1915 (The Phillies lost the series 1-4 to the Red Sox.)

13) D – Whiz Kids (The team consisted of a group of players brought up through the Phillies' farm system. Philadelphia finished with 91 wins and a trip to the World Series for the first time since 1915.)

14) A – Phillie Phanatic (He made his debut with the Phillies on April 25, 1978.)

15) B – False (The official seating capacity is 43,647.)

16) D – Charlie Manuel (He has managed Philadelphia since 2005 and has an all-time record of 354-294 for a .546 winning percentage.)

17) C – Brewers (Philadelphia won the series 3-1 for their first playoff series win since 1993.)

18) B – False (The Phillies have won the NL Pennant six times [1915, 1950, 1980, 1983, 1993, and 2008].)

19) D – Robin Roberts (He pitched 529 career games with the Phillies from 1948-61.)

20) B – Ryan Howard (He led the team with 48 home runs.)

21) C – Athletics (The A's were the original tenants of Shibe Park and played there from 1909 until moving to Kansas City in 1955. The Phillies played at Shibe Park from 1938-70.)

22) B – 2 (The Phillies beat the Orioles in 1980 and Rays in 2008.)

23) A – 799 (Philadelphia was tied for 8th in the league for most runs scored.)

24) B – No (The Phillies finished the season 92-70 for a .568 winning percentage.)

25) D – Mike Schmidt (He won the award in 1980, 1981, and 1986.)

26) C – Blue Jays (The name was chosen in a contest during an effort by new ownership to stimulate interest in the club. Phillies was still maintained as the official nickname during this period.)

27) A – Yes (Philadelphia had a record of 52-44 at the All-Star break for a .542 winning percentage.)

28) A – Ashburn Alley (Named in honor of Phillie great Richie Ashburn, this area features games for the family, granite markers of previous Phillies All-Stars, and a wall of fame that includes bronze plaques of Phillies' greats.)

29) B – No (He played for the Phillies from 1964-67 and again from 1970-71. Bunning was selected as an All-Star in 1964 and 1965.)

30) D – 99 (The last tie game the Phillies played in was against Pittsburgh in 1989.)

31) A – Chase Utley (He won his third straight Silver Slugger in 2008. The award was first presented in 1980. Phillie players have won the award a total of 18 times with Mike Schmidt having won six of them.)

32) C – 1961 (Philadelphia finished 47-101-1.)

33) C – Jim Bunning (He is currently a Senator for Kentucky and was first elected in 1998.)

34) B – 38 (Jimmy Rollins set this record over the 2005-06 seasons. He broke the previous record of 31 set by Ed Delahanty in 1899.)

35) D – Steve Bedrosian (He led the league with 40 saves in 1987 and was awarded the NL Cy Young by the BBWAA.)

36) D – Jamie Moyer (He led all pitchers with 16 wins [16-7].)

37) C – Ed Delahanty (He had 5 at-bats, 5 hits, 4 home runs, and 7 RBIs against Chicago on July 13, 1896. Despite Ed's record breaking effort, Philadelphia lost the game 8-9.)

38) A – Colorado (The Phillies finished 5-0 against the Rockies in 2008.)

39) C – 53 (The last Phillies pitcher to record 20 wins was Steve Carlton in 1982 when he led the league with 23 wins.)

40) A – Whitey (He was given this name because of his very light blond hair.)

41) C – Ryan Howard (He led the team with six RBIs.)

42) A – 0 (The most runs scored by the Phillies in a single season was 944 in 1930.)

43) C – Jim Bunning (He pitched a perfect game against the Mets on June 21, 1964 [Phillies 6, Mets 0]. Bunning only threw 90 pitches in the game.)

44) B – 2 (Brad Lidge [P] and Chase Utley [2B])

45) D – Shane Victorino (He hit a grand slam against the Brewers in game two of the 2008 NL Divisional Series.)

46) C – 5 (This has happened four different times [1976, 1979, 1981, and 1995].)

47) D – 18 (The last manager to last one season or less was Gary Varsho in 2004. He managed just two games and finished 1-1.)

48) B – 38 (The pitching staff went 38-303 during the regular season for a .125 average.)

49) B – Iron Pigs (The team has been affiliated with Philadelphia since 2008 and is a member of the International League.)

50) A – 1962 (The Phillies had an overall record of 14-4 [.777] against the Mets. This was the inaugural season for the New York Mets.)

Note: All answers valid as of the end of the 2008 season, unless otherwise indicated in the question itself.

1) Do the Phillies' uniforms have player numbers on the sleeves?

    A) Yes
    B) No

2) What number did Phillies' great Robin Roberts wear?

    A) 12
    B) 20
    C) 28
    D) 36

3) Not including 2009 inductees, how many players have been inducted into the National Baseball Hall of Fame with the Phillies as their primary team?

    A) 8
    B) 10
    C) 13
    D) 16

4) What was the name of Philadelphia's first home field?

    A) Baker Bowl
    B) Veterans Stadium
    C) Recreation Park
    D) Connie Mack Stadium

Regular Season *2-Point Questions*

5) Did the Phillies have a winning record on the road during the regular season in 2008?

    A) Yes
    B) No

6) How many times did Philadelphia sweep a series during the 2008 regular season?

    A) 3
    B) 6
    C) 8
    D) 10

7) Who broke Chuck Klein's single season home run record with the Phillies?

    A) Ryan Howard
    B) Jim Thome
    C) Dick Allen
    D) Mike Schmidt

8) What team did Charlie Manuel manage before the Phillies?

    A) Cleveland
    B) Minnesota
    C) Detroit
    D) Florida

Regular Season *2-Point Questions*

9) Steve Carlton was a left-handed pitcher.

    A) True
    B) False

10) Which NL opponent have the Phillies played the fewest number of times during the regular season?

    A) Arizona
    B) Colorado
    C) Milwaukee
    D) San Diego

11) What is Philadelphia's all-time regular-season winning percentage against the Dodgers?

    A) .439
    B) .491
    C) .532
    D) .557

12) Since 1950, how many Phillie pitchers have led the league in saves?

    A) 1
    B) 2
    C) 4
    D) 5

13) How many times have Phillie pitchers been awarded the Cy Young Award?

    A) 2
    B) 4
    C) 6
    D) 8

14) What year was Philadelphia's first-ever winning season?

    A) 1885
    B) 1890
    C) 1896
    D) 1902

15) What is the Phillies' record for most hits as a team in a single season?

    A) 1,496
    B) 1,588
    C) 1,641
    D) 1,783

16) Who holds the Phillies' record for most grand slams in a season?

    A) Ryan Howard
    B) Vince DiMaggio
    C) Mike Schmidt
    D) Dick Allen

17) What is the Philadelphia record for fewest errors as a team during the regular season?

    A) 81
    B) 97
    C) 112
    D) 120

18) Which Phillies pitcher had the lowest ERA in 2008 (minimum 50 innings pitched)?

    A) Kyle Kendrick
    B) Chad Durbin
    C) Brad Lidge
    D) Jamie Moyer

19) How many Philadelphia players have been walked 125 times or more in a single season?

    A) 1
    B) 3
    C) 5
    D) 7

20) The Phillies have won greater than 10,000 all-time regular-season games.

    A) True
    B) False

21) What are the most runs scored by the Phillies in a nine-inning game?

    A) 18
    B) 22
    C) 26
    D) 29

22) When was the last time the Phillies turned a triple play?

    A) 2001
    B) 2003
    C) 2005
    D) 2007

23) What was the salary paid to Grover Alexander by the Phillies in 1917?

    A) $12,000
    B) $18,000
    C) $25,000
    D) $32,000

24) Did the Phillies have a Gold Glove winner in 2008?

    A) Yes
    B) No

Regular Season *2-Point Questions*

25) Who was Philadelphia's manager in their first-ever game?

    A) Bill Purcell
    B) Hugh Duffy
    C) Bob Ferguson
    D) Arthur Irwin

26) Who is the current Phillies' pitching coach?

    A) Davey Lopes
    B) Rich Dubee
    C) Milt Thompson
    D) Sam Perlozzo

27) What was the nickname of the 1983 Philadelphia team?

    A) Grand Dads
    B) Old Timers
    C) Geezers
    D) Wheeze Kids

28) Who is the only Philadelphia player to be named All-Star MVP?

    A) Johnny Callison
    B) Jimmy Rollins
    C) Chase Utley
    D) Juan Samuel

29) When was the last time a Phillies player won the National League batting title?

  A) 1980
  B) 1993
  C) 1999
  D) 2007

30) Did Philadelphia have a winning record against any opponent in their first-ever season in the league?

  A) Yes
  B) No

31) How many players have played over 2,000 games for the Phillies?

  A) 1
  B) 2
  C) 4
  D) 5

32) Against which NL team do the Phillies have their best all-time winning percentage (min. 500 games played)?

  A) Mets
  B) Pirates
  C) Astros
  D) Cubs

33) Who holds the Phillies' record for most strikeouts in a single nine-inning game?

    A) Curt Schilling
    B) Steve Carlton
    C) Cole Hamels
    D) Art Mahaffey

34) In which year did the Phillies first face the Dodgers in the playoffs?

    A) 1956
    B) 1969
    C) 1977
    D) 1980

35) What are the most runs allowed by the Phillies in a single game?

    A) 20
    B) 23
    C) 25
    D) 28

36) Robin Roberts had more 20-wins seasons than Steve Carlton.

    A) True
    B) False

Regular Season *2-Point Questions*

37) Who was Philadelphia's first-ever opponent in Citizens Bank Park?

    A) Cincinnati
    B) New York
    C) Atlanta
    D) Pittsburgh

38) How many times has a Phillies player hit for the cycle (Single, Double, Triple, Home Run in the same game)?

    A) 5
    B) 8
    C) 11
    D) 15

39) Which Phillies pitcher holds the Philadelphia record for the lowest ERA in a season?

    A) Tug McGraw
    B) Curt Schilling
    C) Grover Alexander
    D) Robin Roberts

40) Has any Phillies player had a batting average of .400 or higher for a single season?

    A) Yes
    B) No

41) Who holds the Phillies' career record for stolen bases?

    A) Pete Rose
    B) Juan Samuel
    C) Jimmy Rollins
    D) Sherry Magee

42) Has any Philadelphia player ever won the All-Star Home Run Derby?

    A) Yes
    B) No

43) What is the nickname of the AA team affiliated with Philadelphia?

    A) R-Phils
    B) Threshers
    C) Blue Claws
    D) Phillies

44) How many times have the Phillies been swept in the World Series?

    A) 0
    B) 1
    C) 2
    D) 3

Regular Season *2-Point Questions*

45) How many different numbers did Chuck Klein wear while playing for the Phillies?

    A) 1
    B) 3
    C) 5
    D) 7

46) When did the Phillies last host the All-Star game?

    A) 1989
    B) 1996
    C) 2001
    D) 2007

47) How many players had their jersey retired by the Phillies?

    A) 2
    B) 4
    C) 6
    D) 8

48) Who is the only Phillies manager to be named National League Manager of the Year more than once?

    A) Eddie Sawyer
    B) Larry Bowa
    C) Jim Fregosi
    D) Gene Mauch

Regular Season 2-Point Questions

PHILLIEOLOGY TRIVIA CHALLENGE

49) In what decade did the Phillies have the best winning
percentage during the regular season?

    A) 1890s
    B) 1930s
    C) 1970s
    D) 2000s

50) How many Philadelphia players have won the World
Series MVP Award?

    A) 0
    B) 1
    C) 2
    D) 4

PHILADELPHIA PHILLIES BASEBALL

Regular Season Phillies Cool Fact

Like most teams, the Phillies have had various uniform changes over the years. One of the most drastic changes took place in 1979. The front office determined there would be a special uniform used for Saturday games. The uniform would be all burgundy with white stripes down the sides and were to be called "Saturday Night Specials". The uniforms were worn for one game and the fan reaction was very negative. Most fans thought that the players looked like they had on pajamas. The front office quickly retired the uniform and it was never again used as a team uniform. However, Mike Schmidt was granted permission by the Phillies to use the uniform during the 1979 MLB All-Star tour of Japan.

Regular Season Answer Key

1) A – Yes (Philadelphia is the only team in the league to wear the number on the sleeve.)

2) D – 36 (Roberts pitched for the Phillies from 1948-61.)

3) B – 10 (Grover Alexander [1938], Ed Delahanty [1945], Billy Hamilton [1961], Dave Bancroft [1971], Sam Thompson [1974], Robin Roberts [1976], Chuck Klein [1980], Steve Carlton [1994], Richie Ashburn [1995], and Mike Schmidt [1995])

4) C – Recreation Park (The Phillies played here from 1883-86. It was located on the corner of 23rd Street and Ridge Avenue.)

5) A – Yes (Philadelphia finished 44-37 on the road for a .543 winning percentage.)

6) D – 10 (The Phillies swept the Braves [3], Nationals [2], Dodgers [2], Rockies [2], and Brewers during the regular season.)

7) D – Mike Schmidt (Klein set the club record with 43 home runs in 1929. The record stood for 50 years until broken by Schmidt with 45 home runs in 1979.)

8) A – Cleveland (Manuel led the Indians to a record of 220-190 [.537] from 2000-02.)

9) A – True (Carlton played for the Phillies from 1972-86.)

10) C – Milwaukee (The Phillies have played the Brewers a total of 77 times [45-32]. Milwaukee was switched to the NL in 1998.)

11) A – .439 (The Phillies are 887-1,133-10 all-time against the Dodgers.)

12) B – 2 (Jim Konstanty led the league with 22 saves in 1950 and Steve Bedrosian led the league with 40 saves in 1987.)

13) C – 6 (Steve Carlton [1972, 1977, 1980, and 1982], John Denny [1983], and Steve Bedrosian [1987])

14) A – 1885 (Philadelphia finished 56-54-1 for a .509 winning percentage.)

15) D – 1,783 (The Phillies set this record in 1930 after playing just 156 games.)

16) B – Vince DiMaggio (He recorded four grand slams during the 1945 regular season.)

17) A – 81 (This record was set in 2004.)

18) C – Brad Lidge (He pitched 69.1 innings and led the team with a 1.95 ERA.)

19) C – 5 (Richie Ashburn [125 walks, 1954], Billy Hamilton [126 walks, 1894] Bobby Abreu [127 walks, 2004], Mike Schmidt [128 walks, 1983], and Lenny Dykstra [129 walks, 1993])

20) B – False (The Phillies all-time regular-season record is 8,945-10,098-109 for a .470 winning percentage.)

21) C – 26 (The Phillies had 27 hits and beat the Mets 26-7 in 8 ½ innings on June 11, 1985.)

22) D – 2007 (The Phils turned a triple play against the Rockies on Sept. 12, 2007. This was the 30th triple play in franchise history.)

23) A – $12,000 (Alexander first played for the Phillies from 1911-17 leading the league in wins for 5 of those 7 years. In 2008 dollars, his contract would have been worth $203,000. The 2009 league minimum salary is $400,000.)

24) A – Yes (Shortstop Jimmy Rollins won his second Gold Glove and outfielder Shane Victorino won his first.)

25) C – Bob Ferguson (He managed the Phillies the first 17 games, but was replaced by Bill Purcell after going 4-13 [.235]. Purcell was replaced following the season after finishing 13-68-1 [.165].)

26) B – Rich Dubee (2008 marked Dubee's fourth season as Phillies pitching coach.)

27) D – Wheeze Kids (With an aging roster, that included three starters over 40 years old and Steve Carlton who was 38, the Phillies won the NLCS before falling to the Orioles in the World Series.)

28) A – Johnny Callison (He won the award in 1964 after hitting a home run with two RBIs in the 9th inning.)

29) B – 1993 (Lenny Dykstra led the league with 194 hits.)

30) B – No (The Phillies faced seven different teams in 1883 and had a losing record to every team. The best winning percentage was against the Buffalo Bisons [5-9, .357] and the worst was against the Boston Beaneaters [0-14, currently the Atlanta Braves].)

31) A – 1 (Mike Schmidt played 2,404 games with the Phillies. He played his entire career in Philadelphia.)

32) A – Mets (The Phillies are 426-375-1 all-time against New York for a .532 winning percentage.)

33) D – Art Mahaffey (He recorded 17 strikeouts with one walk and four hits against the Cubs in 1961 [Phillies 6, Cubs 0].)

34) C – 1977 (The Phillies lost the NLCS 1-3.)

35) D – 28 (Philadelphia fell 6-28 to the Cardinals on July 6, 1929.)

36) A – True (Roberts recorded six 20-win seasons [1950-55] to Carlton's five [1972, 1976, 1977, 1980, and 1982].)

37) A – Cincinnati (The Phillies lost 1-4 to the Reds in the inaugural game at the new stadium on April 12, 2004.)

38) B – 8 (Lave Cross [1894], Sam Thompson [1894], Cy Williams [1927], Chuck Klein [1931 and 1933], Johnny Callison [1963], Gregg Jefferies [1995], and David Bell [2004])

39) C – Grover Alexander (He had an ERA of 1.22 in 1915 after pitching 376.1 innings and 36 complete games for the season.)

40) A – Yes (Sam Thompson had a .404 average in 1894 and Ed Delahanty had a .408 average in 1899.)

41) D – Sherry Magee (He had 387 stolen bases from 1904-14.)

42) A – Yes (Bobby Abreu won the derby in 2005 with 41 total home runs and Ryan Howard won in 2006 with 23 total home runs. The home run derby started in 1985.)

43) A – R-Phils (The Reading Phillies have been affiliated with Philadelphia since 1967 and compete in the Eastern League.)

44) B – 1 (The Phillies were swept by the Yankees in the 1950 World Series.)

45) D – 7 (Klein played for Philadelphia from 1928-33, 1936-39, and 1940-44. During his playing days for the Phillies he wore numbers 1, 3, 8, 26, 29, 35, and 36.)

46) B – 1996 (The NL beat the AL 6-0 at Veterans Stadium. Philadelphia has hosted the MLB All-Star game four times [1943, 1952, 1976, and 1996]. The NL has a 3-1 record in those games with the only loss coming in 1943.)

47) D – 8 (Rich Ashburn [#1], Jim Bunning [#14], Mike Schmidt [#20], Steve Carlton [#32], Robin Roberts [#36], Jackie Robinson [#42], Grover Cleveland, and Chuck Klein. Every team in Major League Baseball retired Robinson's number in 1997, the 50th anniversary of him becoming the first black player in the league.)

48) D – Gene Mauch (He won the award in 1962 and 1964. Other managers to win the award are Eddie Sawyer [1950], Danny Ozark [1976], Jim Fregosi [1993], and Larry Bowa [2001].)

49) A – 1890s (Philadelphia had an overall record of 743-629-15 during the decade for a .541 winning percentage.)

50) C – 2 (Mike Schmidt [1980] and Cole Hamels [2008])

Note: All answers valid as of the end of the 2008 season, unless otherwise indicated in the question itself.

1) Has any Philadelphia player hit an inside-the-park grand slam?

    A) Yes
    B) No

2) What can be seen behind right center field at Citizens Bank Park?

    A) Scoreboard
    B) Largest American Flag in Pennsylvania
    C) Neon Liberty Bell
    D) Silhouette of Philadelphia Skyline

3) When was the most recent season the Phillies failed to finish over .500?

    A) 1999
    B) 2002
    C) 2004
    D) 2006

4) Which Phillies manager has the most career wins?

    A) Charlie Manuel
    B) Danny Ozark
    C) Jim Fregosi
    D) Gene Mauch

Playoffs

PHILLIEOLOGY TRIVIA CHALLENGE

5) Who was the last Philadelphia pitcher to throw a no-hitter?

    A) Jon Lieber
    B) Randy Wolf
    C) Kevin Millwood
    D) Curt Schilling

6) Which of the following positions is not represented by a Phillie in the National Baseball Hall of Fame?

    A) Shortstop
    B) Third Base
    C) Catcher
    D) Left Fielder

7) What is the best career winning percentage of a Phillies pitcher with at least 100 wins?

    A) .549
    B) .577
    C) .590
    D) .676

8) What is the record for the most pitchers used by the Phillies in a single season?

    A) 20
    B) 22
    C) 25
    D) 28

PHILADELPHIA PHILLIES BASEBALL

Playoffs

9) Against which NL opponent does Philadelphia have the worst regular-season winning percentage?

    A) Giants
    B) Reds
    C) Cubs
    D) Astros

10) What is the current distance to the center field wall at Citizens Bank Park?

    A) 390'
    B) 398'
    C) 401'
    D) 409'

11) Which of the following Phillies' career records is not held by Robin Roberts?

    A) Games Pitched
    B) Complete Games
    C) Games Started
    D) Innings Pitched

12) Which manager holds the Phillies' record for the best winning percentage in postseason play?

    A) Dallas Green
    B) Charlie Manuel
    C) Danny Ozark
    D) Jim Fregosi

Playoffs

PHILLIEOLOGY TRIVIA CHALLENGE

13) What is the Philadelphia record for most errors committed as a team in a single season?

    A) 341
    B) 379
    C) 403
    D) 422

14) Which Phillies pitcher did not win a Gold Glove?

    A) Curt Schilling
    B) Bobby Shantz
    C) Jim Kant
    D) Steve Carlton

15) Is there a statue of Mike Schmidt outside of Citizens Bank Park?

    A) Yes
    B) No

16) How many players have recorded over 250 career stolen bases as a Phil?

    A) 2
    B) 4
    C) 6
    D) 8

PHILADELPHIA PHILLIES BASEBALL

Playoffs

17) Who was the last Phillies player to be named the National League Home Run Champion?

    A) Bobby Abreu
    B) Greg Luzinski
    C) Jim Thome
    D) Ryan Howard

18) What are the most home runs Jimmy Rollins hit in a season with the Phillies?

    A) 26
    B) 30
    C) 34
    D) 39

19) When was the last season Philadelphia failed to have a player record 100 or more RBIs?

    A) 1997
    B) 2000
    C) 2003
    D) 2005

20) Steve Carlton threw more wild pitches as a Phillie than Chris Short and Robin Roberts combined.

    A) True
    B) False

21) Who was the last Phillies pitcher to lead the team in strikeouts, wins, innings pitched, and ERA in the same season?

    A) Cole Hamels
    B) Curt Schilling
    C) Kevin Millwood
    D) Brett Myers

22) Which Philadelphia manager has the best winning percentage (minimum 3 seasons)?

    A) Harry Wright
    B) Bill Shettsline
    C) Steve O'Neill
    D) Dallas Green

23) Greg Luzinski is the last Phillie to start as the left fielder in the MLB All-Star Game.

    A) True
    B) False

24) What was the Phillies' team batting average for the 2008 regular season?

    A) .255
    B) .267
    C) .273
    D) .288

25) Did Chuck Klein end his career with the Phillies?

    A) Yes
    B) No

26) Which Phillie won the most career batting titles?

    A) Chuck Klein
    B) Ed Delahanty
    C) Lenny Dykstra
    D) Richie Ashburn

27) What is the Phillies' record for largest deficit overcome in a victory?

    A) 9
    B) 11
    C) 13
    D) 15

28) Who did the Phillies play on opening day in 2008?

    A) Cincinnati
    B) New York
    C) Chicago
    D) Washington

Playoffs

PHILLIEOLOGY TRIVIA CHALLENGE

29) Tug McGraw holds the Phillies' franchise career record for saves.

   A) True
   B) False

30) Who was the last Phillies player-manager?

   A) Ben Chapman
   B) Gavvy Cravath
   C) Stuffy McInnis
   D) Jimmy Wilson

31) Where did the Phillies play before Citizens Bank Park?

   A) Memorial Stadium
   B) Liberty Ball Park
   C) Philadelphia Field
   D) Veterans Stadium

32) What are the most consecutive losses the Phillies ever had in one season?

   A) 19
   B) 23
   C) 27
   D) 30

33) Who is the only player to hit greater than five home runs in the postseason for the Phillies?

    A) Ryan Howard
    B) Gary Mathews
    C) Bake McBride
    D) Lenny Dykstra

34) What are the Phillies' fewest losses in one season?

    A) 43
    B) 57
    C) 61
    D) 65

35) Have the Phillies ever had two different players hit 35 or more home runs in the same season?

    A) Yes
    B) No

36) Which player holds the Phillies' record for most games in a season with an at-bat?

    A) Doug Glanville
    B) Dave Cash
    C) Chuck Klein
    D) Jimmy Rollins

PHILLIEOLOGY TRIVIA CHALLENGE

37) Who was Philadelphia's first round draft pick in 2008?

A) Zachary Collier
B) Anthony Hewitt
C) Jason Knapp
D) Anthony Gose

38) Who holds the Phillies' record for runs scored in a career?

A) Chuck Klein
B) Richie Ashburn
C) Mike Schmidt
D) Ed Delahanty

39) Grover Alexander is the only Phillies' pitcher to win the National League Triple Crown (wins, strikeouts, ERA).

A) True
B) False

40) When was the last season the Phillies did not have a player hit over .300 (minimum 500 at-bats)?

A) 2001
B) 2003
C) 2005
D) 2008

Playoffs

PHILLIEOLOGY TRIVIA CHALLENGE

41) What is the Phillies' record for the shortest game ever played?

    A) 51 minutes
    B) 1 hour 18 minutes
    C) 1 hour 29 minutes
    D) 1 hour 40 minutes

42) What is the Phillies' record for most innings played in a single game?

    A) 17
    B) 19
    C) 21
    D) 23

43) Did Charlie Manuel ever play for the Phillies?

    A) Yes
    B) No

44) Which Phillies pitcher hit a home run in the 2008 World Series?

    A) Joe Blanton
    B) Cole Hamels
    C) Brett Myers
    D) Jamie Moyer

PHILADELPHIA PHILLIES BASEBALL

45) What is on the back of Phillie Phanatic's jersey?

- A) #1
- B) Liberty Bell
- C) Star
- D) Phillies

46) What color are the letters over the main gate entrance at Citizens Bank Park that spell "Phillies"?

- A) Red
- B) Blue
- C) White
- D) Black

47) What famous college football matchup was held at Veterans Stadium seventeen different years?

- A) Harvard-Yale
- B) Princeton-Columbia
- C) Notre Dame-Army
- D) Army-Navy

48) How many Phillies players have won the Roberto Clemente Award?

- A) 1
- B) 2
- C) 4
- D) 5

Playoffs

49) The Phillies had a better batting average against right-handed pitchers than left-handed pitchers in 2008.

- A) True
- B) False

50) Who hit the first-ever home run for the Phillies at Citizens Bank Park?

- A) Mike Lieberthal
- B) Placido Polanco
- C) David Bell
- D) Bobby Abreu

Playoffs Phillies Cool Fact

The July 13, 1985 game with the Mets marked a record-setting day for the Phillies. They scored a franchise-record 26 runs and this was the first time the team scored 20 or more runs at home in over 75 years. The 26 runs were scored on a total of 27 hits. Von Hayes was the only Phillie to homer in the game. He led off with a single home run in the first and hit a grand slam later in the first to help give the Phils a 9-0 lead. The Phillies hit .540 as a team and recorded ten doubles and two triples on the day. There were only 22,591 fans in attendance that day and it would be another 15 years before Phillie fans would witness their team have a scoring barrage of 20 or more runs at home.

Playoffs Answer Key

1) A – Yes (Four players have hit inside-the-park grand slams: Ted Kazanski [1956], Willie Jones [1951], George Harper [1924], and Irish Meusel [1918].)

2) C – Neon Liberty Bell (The bell swings and rings after every Phillies home run.)

3) B – 2002 (The Phils finished 80-81 for a .497 winning percentage.)

4) D – Gene Mauch (645 wins from 1973-79)

5) C – Kevin Millwood (He pitched a no-hitter against San Francisco on April 27, 2003 with three walks and 10 strikeouts [Phillies 1, SF 0].)

6) C – Catcher (First base and second base are also not represented in the Hall of Fame by a Phillie.)

7) D – .676 (Grover Alexander finished with a career record of 190-91.)

8) D – 28 (The Phillies used 28 pitchers in 2007 and finished the season with a record of 89-73.)

9) A – Giants (The Phillies are 900-1,227 all-time against the Giants for a .423 winning percentage.)

10) C – 401' (The wall is 6' high at straight center field.)

11) C – Games Started (This career record is held by Steve Carlton with 499 games. Roberts holds the other three records: games pitched [529], complete games [272], and innings pitched [3,739.1].)

12) B – Charlie Manuel (He has an overall postseason record of 11-6 [.647] as a Phillies manager.)

13) C – 403 (The Phillies committed 403 errors in 155 games in 1904 for a 2.6 per game average.)

14) A – Curt Schilling (Three Phillie pitchers have been named Gold Glove winners: Bobby Shantz [1964], Jim Kant [1976, 1977], and Steve Carlton [1981].)

15) A – Yes (A statue of Mike Schmidt is located outside of the third base gate. Statues of Richie Ashburn [Ashburn Alley], Steve Carlton [left field gate], and Robin Roberts [first base gate] can also be found at Citizens Bank Park.)

16) C – 6 (Billy Hamilton [508], Ed Delahanty [411], Sherry Magee [387], Jimmy Rollins [295], Larry Bowa [288], and Bobby Abreu [254])

17) D – Ryan Howard (He led the league with 58 home runs in 2006.)

18) B – 30 (He hit a career-high 30 home runs in 2007.)

19) B – 2000 (Scott Rolen led the team with 89 RBIs.)

20) A – True (Carlton threw 120 wild pitches during his 15 year career with the Phillies. Roberts [25 from 1948-61] and Short [71 from 1959-71] combined for 96 over a total of 28 years.)

21) D – Brett Myers (He led the team in 2006 with 12 wins, 198.0 innings pitched, 189 strikeouts, and an ERA of 3.91.)

22) D – Dallas Green (He had an overall record of 169-130 from 1979-81 for a .5652 winning percentage.)

23) A – True (Luzinski was the starting left fielder in the 1978 All-Star Game. Every other position has had a starter since 1993.)

24) A – .255 (The Phillies had 1,407 hits on 5,509 at-bats.)

25) A – Yes (Klein played with the Phillies from 1928-33, 1936-39, and 1940-44. He played with the Cubs from 1934-36 and the Pirates for part of the 1939 season.)

26) C – Richie Ashburn (He led the league in hits three times [221 in 1951, 205 in 1953, and 215 in 1958].)

27) B – 11 (The Phillies overcame an eleven-run deficit after four innings to beat the Cubs 18-16 in ten innings on April 17, 1976.)

28) D – Washington (The Phillies lost 6-11 to the Nationals on opening day.)

29) B – False (McGraw had 94 career saves as a Phillie. Three players had more career saves: Jose Mesa [112], Steve Bedrosian [103], and Mitch Williams [102].)

30) A – Ben Chapman (He played for the Phillies from 1945-46 and managed the team from 1945-48. The Phillies have had a total of 12 player-managers.)

31) D – Veterans Stadium (Commonly referred to as "The Vet", the Phillies played here from 1971-2003.)

32) B – 23 (The Phillies lost every game from July 29, 1961 through the first of a double header on Aug. 20, 1961 finishing the season with a record of 41-101-1 for a .306 winning percentage.)

33) D – Lenny Dykstra (He hit two home runs in the 1993 NLCS and four in the 1993 World Series.)

34) A – 43 (The Phillies finished 71-43-5 in 1886 for a .618 winning percentage.)

35) A – Yes (Greg Luzinski [39] and Mike Schmidt [38] both surpassed the 35 home run mark in 1977.)

36) D – Jimmy Rollins (He set the franchise record and led the league in 2007 with 716 at-bats.)

37) B – Anthony Hewitt (The Phillies picked the SS from Salisbury [Conn.] School with the 24th pick overall.)

38) C – Mike Schmidt (He had 1,506 runs with the Phillies.)

39) B – False (Alexander won the Triple Crown from 1915-17. Steve Carlton is the only other Phillies pitcher to win the Triple Crown [1972].)

40) C – 2005 (Chase Utley led the team with 158 hits on 543 at-bats for a .291 batting average.)

41) A – 51 minutes (The Phillies lost 1-6 to the Giants in the first game of a double header on Sept. 28, 1919.)

42) C – 21 (The Phillies lost 1-2 to the Cubs on July 7, 1918.)

43) B – No (He played as a left fielder for the Twins from 1969-72 and for the Dodgers from 1974-75.)

44) A – Joe Blanton (He hit a home run in the bottom of the fifth with two outs to put the Phillies up 2-0 in game four [Phillies 10, Tampa Bay 2].)

45) C – Star (Phanatic is written across the top with a big star in place of a number.)

46) A – Red (Red letters on a white background with blue stars dotting both i's)

47) D – Army-Navy (Seventeen games were played at the Vet from 1980-2001 [Army went 11-5-1].)

48) B – 2 (Greg Luzinski won the award in 1978 and Garry Maddox won in 1986. The award is given annually to those who exemplify sportsmanship and show positive contributions to their community.)

49) B – False (The Phillies batted .330 against right-handed pitchers and .337 against left-handed pitchers.)

50) D – Bobby Abreu (He scored the Phillies only run against the Reds in the inaugural game on April 4, 2004 [Phillies 1, Reds 4].)

Note: All answers valid as of the end of the 2008 season, unless otherwise indicated in the question itself.

1) Who is the only manager inducted into the National Baseball Hall of Fame as a Phillie?

    A) Harry Wright
    B) Gene Mauch
    C) Paul Owens
    D) Bucky Harris

2) Who was the first African-American player to play for the Phillies?

    A) Dick Allen
    B) Teddy Washington
    C) Bill Johnson
    D) John Kennedy

3) What year did the Phillies adopt the current P logo on their baseball cap?

    A) 1975
    B) 1982
    C) 1988
    D) 1992

4) How many years have the Phillies participated in the Dominican Summer League?

    A) 8
    B) 11
    C) 14
    D) 18

5) The scoreboard at Citizens Bank Park measures greater than 3,000 square feet.

    A) True
    B) False

6) Since 1950, which player holds the Philadelphia record for on-base percentage in a single season?

    A) Richie Ashburn
    B) John Kruk
    C) Ryan Howard
    D) Bobby Abreu

7) What is the Phillies' record for consecutive winning seasons?

    A) 5
    B) 7
    C) 9
    D) 12

8) How many teams has Philadelphia played greater than 2,000 times in the regular season?

    A) 3
    B) 5
    C) 7
    D) 9

9) What was the Phillies' longest winning streak of the 2008 regular season?

    A) 5
    B) 7
    C) 9
    D) 11

10) Which player won the most Gold Gloves as a Phillie?

    A) Mike Schmidt
    B) Scott Rolen
    C) Garry Maddox
    D) Manny Trillo

11) How many Phils have been named National League Most Valuable Player?

    A) 3
    B) 5
    C) 7
    D) 10

12) Chuck Klein is the only Phillie to lead the league in runs scored in three different seasons.

    A) True
    B) False

Championship Series *4-Point Questions*

13) How many Phils have a career batting average of .325 or higher?

    A) 1
    B) 3
    C) 5
    D) 7

14) Who threw out the first pitch of the second game of the 1915 World Series between the Phillies and Red Sox?

    A) Queen Elizabeth
    B) Charlie Chapman
    C) Alfred Reach
    D) Woodrow Wilson

15) What is the Phillies' record for most career home runs by a pitcher?

    A) 9
    B) 11
    C) 14
    D) 17

16) The right field foul pole at Citizens Bank Park is farther from home plate than the left field foul pole.

    A) True
    B) False

17) How many Phillie batters have won the National League Triple Crown?

   A) 0
   B) 1
   C) 2
   D) 3

18) Mike Schmidt hit 30 home runs and 100 RBIs in the same season 10 different times.

   A) True
   B) False

19) Which is not a nickname of a Single A team affiliated with the Phillies?

   A) Threshers
   B) Crosscutters
   C) Mud Hens
   D) Blue Claws

20) Who is the only Phillies pitcher to lead the team in strikeouts for ten or more consecutive years?

   A) Steve Carlton
   B) Robin Roberts
   C) Jim Bunning
   D) Greg Gross

21) All-time, how many managers have the Phillies had?

    A) 38
    B) 46
    C) 51
    D) 60

22) What is the Phillies' team record for consecutive scoreless innings pitched?

    A) 30
    B) 35
    C) 39
    D) 41

23) Which Phillies manager has the second best winning percentage (minimum three seasons)?

    A) Steve O'Neill
    B) Harry Wright
    C) Charlie Manuel
    D) Nick Leyva

24) When was the last time two Phillies pitchers combined for 40 or more wins in a single season?

    A) 1962
    B) 1977
    C) 1980
    D) 1993

25) Who is the only Philadelphia player to be hit by pitch greater than 20 times in a single season?

    A) Ed Bouchee
    B) Chase Utley
    C) Aaron Rowand
    D) Scott Rolen

26) Who is "The Voice of the Phillies"?

    A) Harry Kalas
    B) Chris Wheeler
    C) Gary Matthews
    D) Larry Andersen

27) How many times have the Phillies been in first place at the All-Star break?

    A) 5
    B) 7
    C) 10
    D) 12

28) Who is the only Phillie to record 30 home runs and 30 stolen bases in a single season?

    A) Jimmy Rollins
    B) Mike Schmidt
    C) Juan Samuel
    D) Bobby Abreu

29) What decade did the Phillies have the worst winning percentage?

A) 1920s
B) 1940s
C) 1960s
D) 1990s

30) Do the Phillies have an all-time winning record in interleague play?

A) Yes
B) No

31) Who holds the Phillies' record for most times striking out in a single season?

A) Ivan DeJesus
B) Jim Thome
C) Ryan Howard
D) Greg Luzinski

32) When was the last time an opposing pitcher threw a no-hitter against the Phils?

A) 1978
B) 1982
C) 1995
D) 2002

Championship Series *4-Point Questions*

33) Which pitcher holds the Phillies' career record for most strikeouts?

    A) Jim Bunning
    B) Steve Carlton
    C) Robin Roberts
    D) Grover Alexander

34) Since 1925, what is the Phillie record for most home wins in a single season?

    A) 51
    B) 54
    C) 57
    D) 60

35) Who was the last Phillie to win the BBWAA's National League Rookie of the Year?

    A) Ryan Howard
    B) Scott Rolen
    C) Chase Utley
    D) Shane Victorino

36) How many Phillies have a career slugging percentage of .525 or higher?

    A) 1
    B) 3
    C) 5
    D) 7

37) How many times were the Phillies swept during a series in the 2008 regular season?

A) 1
B) 3
C) 5
D) 7

38) Which Philadelphia World Series team had the worst regular-season winning percentage?

A) 1980
B) 1983
C) 1993
D) 2008

39) Which American League team have the Phillies played the most during the regular season?

A) Boston
B) Oakland
C) Baltimore
D) Cleveland

40) Has a crowd of 70,000 fans or more ever watched a Phillies' home game?

A) Yes
B) No

Championship Series *4-Point Questions*

41) Where do the Phillies hold spring training?

    A) Bradenton, FL
    B) Galveston, TX
    C) Clearwater, FL
    D) Scottsdale, AZ

42) Who was the last Phillies player to lead MLB in batting average (min. 3.1 plate appearances per team game)?

    A) Greg Luzinski
    B) Chase Utley
    C) John Kruk
    D) Richie Ashburn

43) Who holds the Phillie record for consecutive games played?

    A) Richie Ashburn
    B) Ed Delahanty
    C) Jack Baldschun
    D) Dick Allen

44) Which Phillies manager has the second most career wins?

    A) Charlie Manuel
    B) Danny Ozark
    C) Jim Fregosi
    D) Harry Wright

Championship Series *4-Point Questions*

45) What is the Phillies' record for most home runs allowed in a single season?

    A) 190
    B) 214
    C) 231
    D) 249

46) Which player holds the Phillies' record for most RBIs in a single season?

    A) Chuck Klein
    B) Ryan Howard
    C) Mike Schmidt
    D) Pete Rose

47) How many no-hitters have Phillies pitchers thrown?

    A) 5
    B) 7
    C) 9
    D) 11

48) Grover Alexander is the last Phillies pitcher to pitch 30 or more complete games in a single season.

    A) True
    B) False

Championship Series *4-Point Questions*

49) What is the Phillies' all-time record for consecutive wins?

   A) 9
   B) 11
   C) 13
   D) 16

50) Who was the last Phillies outfielder to have 25 or more outfield assists in a single season?

   A) Bobby Abreu
   B) John Callison
   C) Glenn Wilson
   D) Richie Ashburn

Championship Series Phillies Cool Fact

When the Baker Bowl first opened in 1887 as the Phillies new home, it was deemed the finest baseball stadium in America. Although the stadium eventually became an embarrassment, forcing the Phillies to move in 1938 after repairs became too costly, the stadium offers much to Phillies history. It was considered a hitters ballpark. Six of the Phillies' ten Hall of Famers played their entire Phillie careers at Baker Bowl. Babe Ruth made his first appearance in MLB at the Baker Bowl in game one of the 1915 World Series. He also made his last appearance in MLB on May 30, 1935 as a player with the Boston Braves. The Philadelphia Eagles played here from 1933-35, making the Baker Bowl one of the first multi-sport stadiums. The right field measured 280 feet and had a 60-foot wall. An enormous advertisement covered the wall that read "The Phillies use Lifebuoy" (a common soap bar of the time). Since the Phillies finished last or second-to-last in the league 16 of their last 20 years at the Baker Bowl, the phrase "and they still stink" was added to the end of the ad.

Championship Series Answer Key

1) A – Harry Wright (He was inducted into the Hall of Fame as a manager in 1953.)

2) D – John Kennedy (Although Teddy Washington was the first black player to sign with the Phillies in 1954, Kennedy was the first black player to see the field in a Phillies uniform. He played five games in 1957.)

3) D – 1992 (The cap logo has had ten different designs since 1896, even featuring a yellow P from 1938-41.)

4) C – 14 (The Phillies use the league to help develop Latin players.)

5) B – False (The scoreboard measures 39'5" x 69'7" for a total of 2,759 square feet.)

6) A – Richie Ashburn (He had an on-base percentage of .449 in 1955.)

7) C – 9 (The Phils had winning seasons from 1975-83 and had a record of 791-612-2 during that span for a .563 winning percentage.)

8) C – 7 (Braves [1,073-1,174], Cubs [1,077-1,202], Reds [918-1,103], Dodgers [887-1,133], Pirates [1,035-1,180], Cardinals [935-1,193], and Giants [900-1,227])

9) B – 7 (The Phillies won every game from Sept. 11th through Sept. 18th.)

10) A – Mike Schmidt (He won 10 Gold Gloves as a Phillie [1976-84 and 1986].)

11) B – 5 (Chuck Klein [1931 and 1932], Jim Konstanty [1950], Mike Schmidt [1980, 1981, and 1986], Ryan Howard [2006], and Jimmy Rollins [2007])

12) B – False (Billy Hamilton led the league in 1891 [141], 1894 [196], and 1895 [166]. Chuck Klein led the league in 1930 [158], 1931 [121], and 1932 [152].)

13) C – 5 (Billy Hamilton [.361], Ed Delahanty [.348], Elmer Flick [.338], Sam Thompson [.333], and Chuck Klein [.326])

14) D – Woodrow Wilson (This is the first time a President threw out the first pitch in a World Series game.)

15) B – 11 (Larry Christenson and Rick Wise both hit 11 career home runs as pitchers with the Phillies.)

16) A – True (The right field foul pole measures 330' and the left field foul pole measures 329'.)

17) B – 1 (Chuck Klein led the league in 1933 with 28 home runs, 120 RBIs, and a .368 batting average.)

18) B – False (Schmidt accomplished this feat nine different seasons [1974, 1976, 1977, 1979, 1980, 1983, 1984, 1986, and 1987].)

19) C – Mud Hens (The Clearwater [FL] Threshers have been affiliated with the Phillies since 1985, the Lakewood [NJ] Blue Claws since 2001, and the Williamsport [PA] Crosscutters since 2007.)

20) A – Steve Carlton (He led the team in strikeouts thirteen consecutive years from 1972-84. Carlton recorded 2,921 strikeouts during that span.)

21) C – 51 (That is an average of 2.5 years per manager over Philadelphia's 126 year history.)

22) D – 41 (The Phillies pitched 41 consecutive scoreless innings in 1951 with four consecutive shutouts.)

23) A – Steve O'Neill (He had an overall record of 182-140-2 from 1952-54 for a .5648 winning percentage, just .0004 behind Dallas Green.)

24) C – 1980 (Steve Carlton [24] and Dick Ruthven [17])

25) B – Chase Utley (He was hit by pitch 25 times in 2007 and 27 times in 2008.)

26) A – Harry Kalas (He first joined the Phillies' broadcast team in 1971.)

27) C – 10 (1950, 1964, 1974, 1976, 1978, 1993, 1995, 2001, 2004, and 2008]

28) D – Bobby Abreu (He accomplished this in 2001 [31 HRs, 36 SBs] and again in 2004 [30 HRs, 40 SBs].)

29) A – 1920s (Philadelphia had an overall record of 566-962-6 [.371].)

30) B – No (The Phils are 90-109 [.452] in interleague play which first began in 1997.)

31) C – Ryan Howard (He recorded 199 strikeouts in 2007 and again in 2008.)

32) A – 1978 (Bob Forsch threw a no-hitter for St. Louis on April 16th [Phillies 0, STL 5].)

33) B – Steve Carlton (He recorded 3,031 career strikeouts. The next highest is Roberts with 1,871 strikeouts.)

34) D – 60 (The Phils finished 60-21 [.741] at home in 1977.)

35) A – Ryan Howard (He won the award in 2005. Three other Phils have also won the award: Scott Rolen [1997], Richie Allen [1964], and Jack Sanford [1957].)

36) C – 5 (Ryan Howard [.590], Chuck Klein [.553], Dick Allen [.530], Mike Schmidt [.527], and Chase Utley [.526])

37) A – 1 (The only team to sweep the Phillies all season was the Los Angeles Angels.)

38) B – 1983 (The Phillies finished with a 90-72-1 [.556] record during the regular season.)

39) C – Baltimore (The Phillies have an all-time regular season record of 21-21 against the Orioles.)

40) B – No (The most fans to attend a regular-season game was 63,816 on July 3, 1984 against Cincinnati and the most for a postseason game was 67,064 for game five of the 1983 World Series.)

41) C – Clearwater, FL (The Phils have played in Clearwater since 1948.)

42) D – Richie Ashburn (He led the league in 1958 with an average of .350. He also led the league in 1955 [.338] and is the only Phil to have led the league in batting average more than once.)

43) A – Richie Ashburn (He played 730 games from July 7, 1950 through the opener of the 1955 season.)

44) D – Harry Wright (He led the team to a record of 636-566 from 1884-93 [only part of the 1890 season].)

45) B – 214 (This record was set in the 2004 season.)

46) A – Chuck Klein (He recorded 170 RBIs in 1930.)

47) C – 9 (Charles Ferguson [1885], Red Donahue [1898], Charles Fraser [1903], Johnny Lush [1906], Jim Bunning [1964], Rick Wise [1971], Terry Muholland [1990], Tommy Greene [1991], and Kevin Millwood [2003])

48) B – False (Robin Roberts pitched 33 complete games in 1952 and 30 in 1953 and Steve Carlton pitched 30 complete games in 1972.)

49) D – 16 (The Phillies won 16 straight three different seasons: 1887, 1890, and 1892.)

50) B – John Callison (He had 26 outfield assists in 1963.)

Note: All answers valid as of the end of the 2008 season, unless otherwise indicated in the question itself.

Extra Innings Bonus Questions *4-Point Questions*

1) What is the Philadelphia record for most tie games in a single season?

- A) 2
- B) 4
- C) 6
- D) 8

2) All-time, how many World Series games has Philadelphia lost by a single run?

- A) 3
- B) 6
- C) 9
- D) 11

3) How many overall number-one draft picks have the Phillies had?

- A) 1
- B) 3
- C) 5
- D) 7

4) Does Philadelphia have a winning record on opening day?

- A) Yes
- B) No

PHILLIEOLOGY TRIVIA CHALLENGE

5) What are the most wins in a single season by a Phillies pitcher?

    A) 23
    B) 26
    C) 29
    D) 38

6) Since 1932, who is the only Phil to hit 50 or more doubles in a single season?

    A) Mike Schmidt
    B) Richie Ashburn
    C) Bobby Abreu
    D) Chase Utley

7) How many times has Philadelphia finished in first place after the regular season?

    A) 8
    B) 10
    C) 13
    D) 16

8) Philadelphia has more pitchers than outfielders enshrined in the National Baseball Hall of Fame.

    A) True
    B) False

PHILADELPHIA PHILLIES BASEBALL

9) Who did Tug McGraw strike out for the final out of the 1980 World Series?

    A) Jose Cardenal
    B) Frank White
    C) Willie Wilson
    D) George Brett

10) What season did the Phillies play in their first-ever night game?

    A) 1935
    B) 1941
    C) 1948
    D) 1952

Extra Innings Bonus Questions Answer Key

1) D – 8 (The Phillies finished 88-63-8 [.579] in 1913.)

2) D – 11 (Philadelphia lost a total of 19 World Series games, 11 of them by a single run.)

3) A – 1 (Third baseman Pat Burrell became the Phillies first number one overall draft pick in 1998.)

4) B – No (The Phillies are 56-68-2 on opening day for a .452 winning percentage.)

5) D – 38 (Kid Gleason set this record in 1890.)

6) C – Bobby Abreu (He hit 50 doubles in 2002. Chuck Klein holds the record with 59 hit in 1930.)

7) B – 10 (1915, 1950, 1976, 1977, 1978, 1980, 1983, 1993, 2007, and 2008)

8) B – False (Three Phillies pitchers are enshrined [Robin Roberts, Grover Alexander, and Steve Carlton] and four outfielders are enshrined [Sam Thompson, Billy Hamilton, Richie Ashburn, and Ed Delahanty].)

9) C – Willie Wilson (McGraw received the save and Steve Carlton was the winning pitcher.)

10) A – 1935 (The Phillies lost 1-2 to Cincinnati at Crosley Field in the first-ever MLB night game.)

Note: All answers valid as of the end of the 2008 season, unless otherwise indicated in the question itself.

Player / Team Score Sheet

Name:_____

Spring Training		Regular Season		Playoffs		Championship Game		Extra Innings
1	26	1	26	1	26	1	26	1
2	27	2	27	2	27	2	27	2
3	28	3	28	3	28	3	28	3
4	29	4	29	4	29	4	29	4
5	30	5	30	5	30	5	30	5
6	31	6	31	6	31	6	31	6
7	32	7	32	7	32	7	32	7
8	33	8	33	8	33	8	33	8
9	34	9	34	9	34	9	34	9
10	35	10	35	10	35	10	35	10
11	36	11	36	11	36	11	36	
12	37	12	37	12	37	12	37	
13	38	13	38	13	38	13	38	
14	39	14	39	14	39	14	39	
15	40	15	40	15	40	15	40	
16	41	16	41	16	41	16	41	
17	42	17	42	17	42	17	42	
18	43	18	43	18	43	18	43	
19	44	19	44	19	44	19	44	
20	45	20	45	20	45	20	45	
21	46	21	46	21	46	21	46	
22	47	22	47	22	47	22	47	
23	48	23	48	23	48	23	48	
24	49	24	49	24	49	24	49	
25	50	25	50	25	50	25	50	
___ x 1 = ___		___ x 2 = ___		___ x 3 = ___		___ x 4 = ___		___ x 4 = ___

Multiply total number correct by point value/quarter to calculate totals for each quarter.

Add total of all quarters below.

Total Points:_____

Thank you for playing Phillieology Trivia Challenge.
Additional score sheets are available at:
www.TriviaGameBooks.com

85

Player / Team Score Sheet

Name:_____

Spring Training		Regular Season		Playoffs		Championship Game		Extra Innings
1	26	1	26	1	26	1	26	1
2	27	2	27	2	27	2	27	2
3	28	3	28	3	28	3	28	3
4	29	4	29	4	29	4	29	4
5	30	5	30	5	30	5	30	5
6	31	6	31	6	31	6	31	6
7	32	7	32	7	32	7	32	7
8	33	8	33	8	33	8	33	8
9	34	9	34	9	34	9	34	9
10	35	10	35	10	35	10	35	10
11	36	11	36	11	36	11	36	
12	37	12	37	12	37	12	37	
13	38	13	38	13	38	13	38	
14	39	14	39	14	39	14	39	
15	40	15	40	15	40	15	40	
16	41	16	41	16	41	16	41	
17	42	17	42	17	42	17	42	
18	43	18	43	18	43	18	43	
19	44	19	44	19	44	19	44	
20	45	20	45	20	45	20	45	
21	46	21	46	21	46	21	46	
22	47	22	47	22	47	22	47	
23	48	23	48	23	48	23	48	
24	49	24	49	24	49	24	49	
25	50	25	50	25	50	25	50	
___ x 1 = ___		___ x 2 = ___		___ x 3 = ___		___ x 4 = ___		___ x 4 = ___

Multiply total number correct by point value/quarter to calculate totals for each quarter.

Add total of all quarters below.

Total Points:_____

Thank you for playing Phillieology Trivia Challenge.
Additional score sheets are available at:
www.TriviaGameBooks.com

87